Understanding Boys with ADHD

Discover how to love, care and parent
your teen boy with ADHD

Samantha Bennett

Copyright

© 2024 Samantha Bennett

Table of Contents

Introduction

In the close-knit community of Greenwood, there lived a mother named Mrs. Brown, whose world revolved around her vibrant son, Ethan. When the diagnosis of Attention-Deficit/Hyperactivity Disorder (ADHD) entered their lives, Mrs. Brown was faced with a whirlwind of emotions, uncertainties, and a deep-seated determination to support her beloved child.

In the midst of confusion and apprehension, Mrs. Brown stumbled upon a guidebook titled "Understanding Kid Boys with ADHD." This book proved to be a lifeline, offering practical wisdom, illuminating insights, and heartwarming tales of resilience for families navigating similar journeys.

As Mrs. Brown immersed herself in the words of the guidebook, she uncovered a treasure trove of strategies to help manage Ethan's boundless energy, communicate effectively with him, and cultivate a nurturing environment within their home. The guidebook became a trusted companion, empowering Mrs. Brown with the knowledge and compassion needed to navigate the challenges of parenting a child with ADHD.

Through her unwavering dedication and the lessons learned from the guidebook, Mrs. Brown witnessed remarkable growth in Ethan. His self-confidence bloomed, his behaviors evolved, and the bond between mother and son deepened with each passing day. Mrs.Brown's narrative is a testament to the profound impact of understanding, acceptance, and unconditional love in the journey of supporting a child with ADHD.

Understanding ADHD in Children

In the world of children, there is a condition called Attention-Deficit/Hyperactivity Disorder (ADHD) that adds an extra layer of complexity to their experiences. ADHD can make it challenging for children to focus, stay organized, and control their impulses.

When a child has ADHD, they may find it hard to pay attention in school, follow instructions, or sit still for long periods. This can sometimes lead to misunderstandings and frustrations, both for the child and those around them.

Understanding ADHD in children involves recognizing that their brains work differently and that they may need extra support and strategies to thrive. By learning about the symptoms of ADHD, developing patience, and providing structure and consistency, caregivers and educators can help children with ADHD navigate their daily lives more successfully.

It's important to approach children with ADHD with empathy and understanding, acknowledging their challenges while also celebrating their unique strengths and talents. With the right guidance and support, children with ADHD can learn to manage their symptoms, build self-confidence, and reach their full potential in both academic and social settings.

Gender Differences in ADHD Presentation

When it comes to Attention-Deficit/Hyperactivity Disorder (ADHD), there is a fascinating interplay between the experiences of boys and girls. While the core symptoms of ADHD — inattention, impulsivity, and hyperactivity — are common across genders, the way these symptoms manifest and are perceived can vary between boys and girls.

In boys, ADHD often presents with more noticeable externalizing behaviors, such as hyperactivity and impulsivity. Boys with ADHD may be perceived as disruptive in the classroom, struggling to sit still, follow rules, and stay focused on tasks. Their symptoms are more overt and may lead to earlier recognition and diagnosis.

On the other hand, girls with ADHD may exhibit more internalizing behaviors, such as daydreaming, emotional dysregulation, and inattention. Girls are more likely to display symptoms quietly, masking their struggles and flying under the radar. This can result in their ADHD being overlooked or misinterpreted as other conditions, such as anxiety or depression.

The societal expectations and gender stereotypes imposed on boys and girls can also influence the way ADHD presents itself. Boys are often expected to be active and assertive, which can align with the hyperactive and impulsive behaviors seen in ADHD. In contrast, girls are often encouraged to be quiet, compliant, and focused on social relationships, which may mask their ADHD symptoms or lead to misperceptions about their behavior.

Recognizing these gender differences in ADHD presentation is crucial for accurate diagnosis and effective support. By understanding how ADHD may manifest differently in boys and girls, caregivers, educators, and healthcare professionals can provide tailored interventions and accommodations to meet the unique needs of each individual.

Through heightened awareness, empathy, and a holistic approach to ADHD assessment and treatment, we can ensure that both boys and girls receive the support and understanding they need to thrive despite the challenges posed by ADHD. By embracing the nuanced nature of gender differences in ADHD presentation, we pave the way for a more inclusive and compassionate approach to supporting individuals of all genders affected by this complex neurodevelopmental disorder.

Chapter 1: What is ADHD?

ADHD, which stands for Attention-Deficit/Hyperactivity Disorder, is a common neurodevelopmental disorder that affects both children and adults. Individuals with ADHD may have difficulty with attention, impulsivity, and hyperactivity, which can impact their daily lives in various ways.

People with ADHD may struggle to stay focused on tasks, follow instructions, or organize their thoughts. They may also exhibit impulsive behaviors, acting without considering the consequences, and may have difficulty sitting still or waiting their turn.

ADHD is not a result of laziness or a lack of intelligence; rather, it is a neurobiological condition that affects how the brain functions. While the exact cause of ADHD is not fully understood, research suggests that genetics, brain chemistry, and environmental factors may play a role in its development.

The Diagnostic and Statistical Manual of Mental Disorders (DSM-5) has specific criteria that are often used to make the diagnosis of ADHD. Healthcare providers assess symptoms, duration, and the impact of symptoms on daily functioning to determine if an individual meets the criteria for an ADHD diagnosis.

Treatment for ADHD often involves a combination of medication, behavioral therapy, and lifestyle modifications. With proper support and interventions, individuals with ADHD can learn to manage their symptoms, improve concentration, and lead productive lives.

It is important to recognize that ADHD is a complex and multifaceted condition that can vary in severity and presentation from person to person. Seeking a comprehensive understanding of ADHD is key to providing effective support and resources for individuals affected by this disorder.

What Type of ADHD Does Your Son Have?

ADHD can be categorized into three main types: predominantly inattentive type, predominantly hyperactive-impulsive type, and combined type.

1. Predominantly Inattentive Type: If your son has predominantly inattentive ADHD, he may struggle with maintaining focus, following through on tasks, and organizing activities. He might appear forgetful, easily distracted, and disorganized, leading to difficulties in school, work, or daily responsibilities.

2. Predominantly Hyperactive-Impulsive Type: In contrast, if your son has predominantly hyperactive-impulsive ADHD, he may display high levels of energy, restlessness, and

impulsivity. He might have a hard time sitting still, talking excessively, and acting without thinking about the consequences. These behaviors can impact his relationships, academic performance, and self-control.

3. Combined Type: Some individuals with ADHD exhibit symptoms of both inattention and hyperactivity-impulsivity, known as combined type ADHD. If your son has combined type ADHD, he may experience a combination of challenges related to focus, hyperactivity, and impulsivity. This can present a unique set of obstacles that require a comprehensive approach to addressing and managing his symptoms.

Understanding the specific type of ADHD that your son has is important in tailoring interventions and support strategies to meet his individual needs. By identifying his predominant symptoms and behavioral patterns, you can work collaboratively with healthcare professionals, educators, and caregivers to develop a personalized treatment plan that maximizes his potential for success and well-being.

Being aware of the type of ADHD your son has can guide you in advocating for the appropriate resources, accommodations, and therapies that can help him thrive in various aspects of his life. By addressing his specific challenges and building on his strengths, you can support his growth, development, and overall quality of life.

Managing your child's fear

Fear is a natural and common emotion that children may experience in various situations, such as starting a new school, meeting new people, or facing challenges. As a parent, helping your child manage their fear is an important part of supporting their emotional well-being and building their resilience.

1. Acknowledge and Validate Emotions: When your child expresses fear, it is essential to

acknowledge their feelings and let them know that it is okay to feel scared. Validating their emotions creates an environment of trust and open communication, allowing them to express their fears without judgment.

2. Encourage Open Dialogue: Create a safe space for your child to talk about their fears openly. Listen attentively without interrupting, and ask gentle questions to understand their concerns better. Encouraging dialogue helps your child feel supported and understood.

3. Provide Reassurance: Offer reassurance to your child by validating their feelings and providing comfort. Remind them that it is normal to feel scared at times and that you are there to support and guide them through their fears.

4. Teach Coping Strategies: Empower your child with coping strategies to manage their fear, such as deep breathing, positive self-talk, or visualization techniques. Encourage them to

practice these strategies when they feel afraid or anxious, helping them regain a sense of control and calm in challenging situations.

5. Expose Gradually to Fears: When appropriate, gradually expose your child to their fears in a controlled and supportive manner. Start with small steps and provide encouragement as they face their fears, building confidence and resilience over time.

6. Model Healthy Coping: Children often learn by observing their parents' behaviors. Model healthy coping mechanisms for managing fear, such as staying calm, problem-solving, and seeking support when needed. Your example can reinforce positive coping skills in your child.

7. Seek Professional Support if Needed: If your child's fear significantly impacts their daily life or persists over a long period, consider seeking professional guidance from a counselor, therapist, or mental health professional. They

can provide additional resources and strategies to help your child effectively manage their fears.

Chapter 2: Recognizing ADHD in Boys

Attention-Deficit/Hyperactivity Disorder (ADHD) can present differently in boys compared to girls, with boys often exhibiting more noticeable outward symptoms. Recognizing ADHD in boys involves understanding the common signs and behaviors associated with the condition, as well as being aware of the factors that can influence its presentation.

1. Hyperactivity and Impulsivity: Boys with ADHD may display high levels of activity, restlessness, and impulsivity. They may have difficulty sitting still, constantly fidgeting, and acting without considering the consequences of their actions. These behaviors can be disruptive

in social settings and may impact their academic performance.

2. Inattention and Distractibility: Boys with ADHD may struggle with maintaining focus, following instructions, and staying organized. They may appear forgetful, easily distracted, and have difficulty completing tasks that require sustained attention. This inattentiveness can affect their ability to learn and engage in activities.

3. Behavioral Challenges: Boys with ADHD may exhibit challenging behaviors such as defiance, aggression, or difficulty regulating emotions. They may have trouble controlling their impulses and managing their reactions in response to frustration or perceived provocation. Understanding and addressing these behavioral challenges is crucial in supporting boys with ADHD and helping them develop effective coping mechanisms.

4. Academic and Social Difficulties: Boys with ADHD may experience academic challenges, such as poor concentration, forgetfulness, and disorganization, which can impact their school performance. Additionally, they may struggle with social interactions, impulsively interrupting others, or having difficulty waiting their turn in conversations or activities.

5. Environmental Factors: Environmental factors, such as family dynamics, parenting styles, school environment, and social interactions, can influence the expression of ADHD symptoms in boys. Recognizing and addressing these external factors can help create a supportive and conducive environment for boys with ADHD to thrive.

6. Early Intervention and Diagnosis: Early recognition and diagnosis of ADHD in boys are essential for providing timely interventions and support. Consulting with healthcare professionals, educators, and mental health specialists can help assess symptoms, develop a

treatment plan, and implement tailored strategies to address the unique needs of boys with ADHD.

Identifying ADHD Symptoms in Boys

Recognizing the symptoms of Attention-Deficit/Hyperactivity Disorder (ADHD) in boys is essential for early intervention and effective management. Boys with ADHD may exhibit a range of behaviors and challenges that can impact their daily functioning, academic performance, and social interactions.

1. Inattention:
- Difficulty focusing on tasks or activities
- Forgetfulness and frequent errors in schoolwork or chores
- Easily distracted by external stimuli
- Trouble organizing tasks and activities
- Tendency to lose things necessary for tasks

2. Hyperactivity:
- Excessive fidgeting or restlessness
- Difficulty remaining seated when required
- Excessive talking or interrupting conversations
- Impulsivity in actions without considering consequences
- frequently having a "on-the-go" or "motor-driven" sense
3. Impulsivity:
- Acting without thinking about the consequences
- Difficulty waiting for turns in activities or conversations
- Interrupting others during discussions or play
- Making impulsive decisions without considering long-term outcomes
- Engaging in risky behaviors without assessing potential dangers

4. Emotional Regulation:
- Mood swings and emotional outbursts
- Difficulty managing frustration or anger
- Sensitivity to criticism or perceived rejection

- Intense reactions to minor setbacks or disappointments
- Difficulty regulating emotions in social situations

5. School Performance:
- Despite having average or above-average intelligence, poor academic performance
- Challenges with completing homework assignments or projects
- Forgetfulness of tasks or instructions in the classroom
- Difficulty staying organized with school materials and supplies
- Distractibility during lessons or class activities

6. Social Interactions:
- Difficulty maintaining friendships or forming close relationships
- Impulsivity in social interactions, leading to conflicts or misunderstandings
- Interrupting others during conversations or play

- Inability to wait for turns in group activities or games
- Disruptive behavior in social settings, such as excessive talking or inappropriate comments

Challenges Faced by Boys with ADHD

Boys with Attention-Deficit/Hyperactivity Disorder (ADHD) often encounter a variety of challenges that can affect various aspects of their lives. These challenges stem from the core symptoms of ADHD, including inattention, hyperactivity, and impulsivity, and can impact their academic performance, social interactions, and overall well-being. Here are some of the key challenges faced by boys with ADHD:

1. Academic Struggles:
Boys with ADHD may face difficulties in school due to inattention, impulsivity, and poor organization skills. They may have trouble

staying focused during lessons, completing assignments, and following instructions. As a result, their academic performance may suffer, leading to lower grades and increased frustration.

2. Social Interactions:
Boys with ADHD may encounter challenges in social settings, such as making and maintaining friendships. Their impulsivity and difficulty in controlling their behavior can lead to social awkwardness, conflict with peers, and misunderstandings. They may struggle with taking turns, listening attentively, and following social cues, making it harder to connect with others.

3. Emotional Regulation:
Managing emotions can be a significant challenge for boys with ADHD. They may experience intense emotions, such as frustration, anger, or anxiety, and
have difficulty regulating their responses to these feelings. This emotional dysregulation can

lead to outbursts, tantrums, and mood swings, impacting their self-esteem and relationships with others.

4. Executive Functioning:
Executive functioning skills, such as organization, time management, and planning, are often impaired in boys with ADHD. They may struggle with keeping track of deadlines, remembering tasks, and prioritizing activities. This can result in disorganization, forgetfulness, and difficulties in completing everyday tasks efficiently.

5. Impulse Control:
Boys with ADHD often struggle with impulse control, acting on immediate desires without considering consequences. This impulsivity can manifest in risky behaviors, impulsive decision-making, and difficulty in stopping or inhibiting actions. These challenges can lead to accidents, conflicts, and disciplinary issues.

6. Self-Regulation:

Self-regulation, including managing impulses, emotions, and behavior, is a common challenge for boys with ADHD. They may have difficulty controlling their impulses, staying focused on tasks, and regulating their energy levels. This can affect their ability to engage in goal-directed activities and maintain self-control in various situations.

Addressing the challenges faced by boys with ADHD requires a combination of support, understanding, and tailored interventions. By recognizing these difficulties and providing the necessary resources and strategies, parents, educators, and healthcare providers can help boys with ADHD overcome obstacles, build resilience, and thrive in their personal and academic lives.

Chapter 3: Diagnosis and Assessment

Diagnosing Attention-Deficit/Hyperactivity Disorder (ADHD) in children involves a comprehensive evaluation process that considers various factors, including symptoms, behaviors, and developmental history. The assessment is typically conducted by healthcare professionals, such as pediatricians, psychologists, or psychiatrists, who specialize in diagnosing and treating ADHD.

1. Initial Screening:
The evaluation process often begins with an initial screening to assess the child's symptoms and behaviors. Parents, teachers, and caregivers may be asked to complete standardized questionnaires or rating scales that help identify ADHD-related issues, such as inattention, hyperactivity, and impulsivity.

2. Comprehensive Evaluation:

A comprehensive evaluation is conducted to gather information about the child's medical history, developmental milestones, academic performance, and social interactions. The healthcare provider may also observe the child's behavior in various settings, such as home, school, or clinical settings, to assess their symptoms and functioning.

3. Diagnostic Criteria:

The diagnosis of ADHD is based on specific criteria outlined in the Diagnostic and Statistical Manual of Mental Disorders (DSM-5). To meet the criteria for an ADHD diagnosis, the child must exhibit a certain number of symptoms of inattention, hyperactivity, and impulsivity that are persistent, pervasive, and significantly impact their daily life functioning, such as academics, relationships, and daily routines.

4. Differential Diagnosis:

During the assessment process, healthcare providers may consider other conditions that can present similar symptoms to ADHD, such as anxiety disorders, learning disabilities, or sensory processing issues. A differential diagnosis helps ensure that the child receives an accurate and appropriate diagnosis that guides effective treatment strategies.

5. Collaboration and Information Sharing:

Collaboration between healthcare professionals, parents, teachers, and caregivers is essential in the assessment and diagnosis of ADHD. Sharing information about the child's behavior, challenges, and strengths across different settings can provide a more comprehensive understanding of their symptoms and help inform the diagnostic process.

6. Treatment Planning:

Once a diagnosis of ADHD is confirmed, healthcare providers work with the child and their family to develop a personalized treatment plan that addresses their specific needs. Treatment may involve a combination of behavioral therapy, medication, academic accommodations, and lifestyle modifications to help manage symptoms and improve functioning.

7. Ongoing Monitoring and Follow-Up:
After the initial diagnosis, ongoing monitoring and follow-up are important to track the child's progress, adjust treatment strategies as needed, and address any emerging challenges. Regular communication between healthcare providers, educators, and parents helps ensure that the child receives the support and resources necessary to thrive and succeed despite the challenges of ADHD.

How ADHD is Diagnosed in Children

Diagnosing Attention-Deficit/Hyperactivity Disorder (ADHD) in boys involves a comprehensive evaluation process that considers a range of factors to determine if the child meets the diagnostic criteria. The diagnosis of ADHD in boys typically follows a multi-step approach that includes gathering information from various sources, assessing the child's symptoms and behaviors, and considering their developmental history.

1. Initial Screening:
The diagnostic process often begins with an initial screening to assess the child's behavior and symptoms. Standardized questionnaires or rating scales filled out by parents, guardians, teachers, and other people who regularly contact with the child may be used for this.These

screenings help identify potential ADHD-related issues and provide valuable information for further evaluation.

2. Comprehensive Evaluation:
A comprehensive evaluation is conducted by a healthcare professional, such as a pediatrician, psychologist, or psychiatrist, specializing in ADHD diagnosis. This evaluation involves a thorough review of the child's medical history, developmental milestones, academic performance, and social interactions. The healthcare provider may also observe the child's behavior in different settings to assess their symptoms and functioning.

3. Diagnostic Criteria:
The diagnosis of ADHD in boys follows specific criteria outlined in the Diagnostic and Statistical Manual of Mental Disorders (DSM-5), a widely used guide for mental health professionals. To meet the criteria for an ADHD diagnosis, the child must exhibit a certain number of symptoms of inattention, hyperactivity, or impulsivity that

are persistent, pervasive, and significantly impact their daily functioning.

4. Parent and Teacher Input:
Input from parents, caregivers, and teachers is crucial in the diagnostic process. These individuals provide valuable information about the child's behavior, challenges, and strengths in different settings, such as home, school, and social environments. Their insights help paint a comprehensive picture of the child's symptoms and the impact of ADHD on their daily life.

5. Behavioral Observations:
Direct observations of the child's behavior in various contexts are essential for assessing ADHD symptoms. Healthcare providers may observe the child's ability to focus, sustain attention, manage impulses, and interact with others. These observations help corroborate reported symptoms and provide additional insights into the child's functioning.

6. Rule Out Other Conditions:
As part of the diagnostic process, healthcare providers consider other conditions that can mimic or coexist with ADHD. These may include learning disabilities, anxiety disorders, sensory processing issues, or other neurodevelopmental disorders. A thorough evaluation helps differentiate ADHD from other conditions and ensures an accurate diagnosis that guides appropriate treatment and interventions.

7. Collaborative Approach:
Diagnosing ADHD in boys often involves a collaborative approach among healthcare providers, parents, teachers, and other caregivers. Open communication, information sharing, and teamwork are essential for a comprehensive evaluation and accurate diagnosis. Collaborating with multiple stakeholders helps gather diverse perspectives and ensures a holistic understanding of the child's symptoms.

8. Treatment Planning:

Once a diagnosis of ADHD is confirmed, healthcare providers work with the child and their family to develop a personalized treatment plan. This plan may include a combination of behavioral therapies, educational interventions, medication management, and lifestyle adjustments to address the child's specific needs and support their overall well-being.

Home remedy for managing ADHD

While ADHD is a complex neurodevelopmental disorder that often requires professional intervention and treatment, there are some home remedies and strategies that can complement medical care and support the well-being of boys with ADHD. These approaches focus on creating a structured, supportive environment that fosters positive behaviors and helps manage ADHD symptoms. Here is an overview of home remedies for managing boys with ADHD:

1. Consistent Routine:

Establishing a consistent daily routine can help boys with ADHD feel more organized and secure. Set regular times for waking up, meals, homework, playtime, and bedtime. Clear schedules and visual cues, such as calendars or checklists, can help them understand expectations and transition between activities smoothly.

2. Healthy Diet:

Nutritious meals play a crucial role in managing ADHD symptoms. A balanced diet rich in fruits, vegetables, whole grains, and lean proteins can support brain health and improve focus. Limiting processed foods, sugary snacks, and artificial additives may help reduce hyperactivity and impulsivity.

3. Regular Exercise:

Physical activity is beneficial for boys with ADHD as it helps release excess energy, improve focus, and regulate mood. Encourage regular exercise and outdoor play to promote physical activity and reduce stress. Activities such as biking, swimming, running, or team sports can be fun and beneficial for boys with ADHD.

4. Adequate Sleep:

Adequate sleep is essential for children with ADHD to regulate their emotions and maintain focus. Establish a calming bedtime routine, ensure a quiet sleep environment, and limit screen time before bed. Consistent sleep schedules can help boys with ADHD feel rested and better able to manage their symptoms during the day.

5. Mindfulness and Relaxation Techniques:

Teaching boys with ADHD mindfulness and relaxation techniques can help them regulate their emotions and reduce impulsivity. Practices such as deep breathing exercises, progressive muscle relaxation, and guided imagery can promote calmness and focus. Incorporating these techniques into daily routines can support emotional well-being.

6. Limiting Screen Time:
Excessive screen time, including television, video games, and electronic devices, can exacerbate ADHD symptoms in boys. Set limits on screen time, encourage meaningful interactions, and promote alternative activities such as reading, outdoor play, or creative hobbies. Balancing screen time with real-world experiences can help improve attention and behavior.

7. Positive Reinforcement:
Encouraging positive behaviors and accomplishments through praise, rewards, and positive reinforcement can motivate and empower boys with ADHD. Use a reward system to acknowledge and reinforce desired behaviors, such as following instructions,

completing tasks, or controlling impulses. Celebrate small successes and progress to boost self-esteem and confidence.

8. Effective Communication:
Open and honest communication is essential for supporting boys with ADHD. Encourage active listening, validate their feelings, and provide clear, concise instructions. Use positive language, offer encouragement, and engage in constructive problem-solving to foster a positive and supportive home environment.

Tools for Evaluating ADHD Symptoms

When assessing Attention-Deficit/Hyperactivity Disorder symptoms in children, healthcare providers and mental health professionals use a variety of tools and methods to gather information, track behaviors, and make an accurate diagnosis. These evaluation tools help assess the presence and severity of ADHD symptoms, monitor progress, and inform treatment planning.

1. Behavior Rating Scales:

Behavior rating scales are standardized questionnaires completed by parents, teachers, and caregivers to assess a child's behavior in different settings. These scales measure ADHD-related symptoms, such as inattention, hyperactivity, impulsivity, and behavioral challenges. Examples of behavior rating scales include the ADHD Rating Scale and the Behavioral Assessment System for Children (BASC).

2. Vanderbilt Assessment Scale:

The Vanderbilt Assessment Scale is a commonly used tool for evaluating ADHD symptoms in children. It involves a series of questions about a child's behavior, attention, and social interactions, completed by parents and teachers. The scale helps healthcare providers assess the presence and severity of ADHD symptoms and determine the need for further evaluation.

3. Conners Rating Scales:

The Conners Rating Scales are comprehensive assessment tools that measure various aspects of behavior, cognition, and emotional functioning in children with ADHD. These scales include parent, teacher, and self-report versions that assess ADHD symptoms, emotional lability, executive functioning, and social behaviors. The Conners Rating Scales provide valuable information for diagnosing ADHD and developing individualized treatment plans.

4. Continuous Performance Tests (CPTs):

Continuous Performance Tests are computer-based assessments that measure attention, impulsivity, and sustained attention in children with ADHD. CPTs evaluate a child's ability to maintain focus, inhibit responses, and sustain attention over time. These tests provide objective data on cognitive functioning and can help differentiate ADHD from other conditions.

5. Observation Tools:
Direct observation of a child's behavior in different settings, such as home, school, or clinical environments, is an essential evaluation method for assessing ADHD symptoms. Healthcare providers observe the child's interactions, attention span, impulse control, and hyperactivity to gather information about their daily functioning and behavior.

6. Neuropsychological Testing:
Neuropsychological testing involves a comprehensive assessment of cognitive functions, such as attention, memory, executive functioning, and processing speed. These tests provide detailed information about a child's cognitive strengths and weaknesses, helping identify underlying cognitive deficits that may contribute to ADHD symptoms.

7. Diagnostic Interviews:
Diagnostic interviews with parents, caregivers, and teachers are important tools for gathering detailed information about a child's

developmental history, symptoms, behaviors, and social functioning. These interviews help healthcare providers understand the child's challenges, strengths, and the impact of ADHD symptoms on their daily life.

8. Psychological Assessments:
Psychological assessments, including IQ testing, academic achievement tests, and social-emotional assessments, can provide additional information about a child's cognitive abilities, academic performance, and emotional well-being. These assessments complement the evaluation process and help identify areas of strength and areas needing support.

Chapter 4: Treatment Approaches

Managing this Disorder in children involves a multimodal treatment approach that combines various strategies to address symptoms, enhance functioning, and improve overall well-being. Treatment for ADHD typically includes a combination of behavioral interventions, medication management, academic support, and lifestyle modifications tailored to the individual needs of the child.

1. Behavioral Therapy:
Behavioral therapy is a cornerstone of ADHD treatment, focusing on teaching children skills to manage their symptoms, improve self-control, and enhance social interactions. Behavior therapy techniques, such as behavior modification, parent training, and social skills training, help children develop coping strategies,

improve impulse control, and regulate their emotions effectively.

2. Medication Management:

Medication is often prescribed as part of ADHD treatment to manage symptoms such as inattention, hyperactivity, and impulsivity. Stimulant medications, such as methylphenidate (Ritalin) or amphetamine-based drugs (Adderall), are commonly used to improve focus and self-control in children with ADHD. Non-stimulant medications, such as atomoxetine (Strattera) or guanfacine (Intuniv), may be recommended for children who exhibit moderate to severe symptoms or do not respond well to stimulant medications. Medication management should be closely monitored by healthcare providers to ensure effectiveness and address any potential side effects.

3. Academic Accommodations:

Children with ADHD may benefit from academic accommodations and support in school to help them succeed academically. These accommodations may include extended time on tests, preferential seating, frequent breaks, and modified assignments. Individualized Education Plans (IEPs) or 504 plans can outline specific accommodations and services to meet the child's educational needs.

4. Parent and Teacher Involvement:
Involving parents and teachers in the treatment process is crucial for supporting children with ADHD. Collaborating with parents to implement behavioral strategies at home and communicating with teachers to address academic challenges and behavioral issues in the classroom can enhance treatment outcomes and support the child's overall development.

5. Cognitive-Behavioral Therapy (CBT):
Cognitive-behavioral therapy focuses on identifying and changing negative thought patterns and behaviors that contribute to ADHD symptoms. CBT helps children develop problem-solving skills, improve self-esteem, and manage stress, enhancing their ability to cope

with challenges and regulate their emotions effectively.

6. Lifestyle Modifications:
Healthy lifestyle modifications can have a positive impact on managing ADHD symptoms. Encouraging regular exercise, adequate sleep, and a balanced diet can improve focus, mood, and overall well-being in children with ADHD. Limiting screen time, promoting outdoor play, and creating a structured routine can also support symptom management and enhance cognitive functioning.

7. Support Groups and Counseling:
Support groups and counseling services provide children with ADHD and their families opportunities to connect with others facing similar challenges, share experiences, and learn coping strategies. Individual or family counseling can help address emotional issues, improve communication, and build resilience in children with ADHD and their families.

8. Mindfulness and Relaxation Techniques:
Teaching children mindfulness and relaxation techniques, such as deep breathing exercises, meditation, and visualization, can help reduce stress, improve focus, and enhance self-regulation. These techniques promote calmness, emotional balance, and increased self-awareness, which can benefit children with ADHD in managing their symptoms effectively.

positive reinforcement techniques

Positive reinforcement techniques play a significant role in managing behaviors and supporting the development of children, especially those with Attention-Deficit/Hyperactivity Disorder (ADHD). Implementing positive reinforcement strategies tailored to the specific needs of boys with ADHD can help enhance their self-esteem, motivation, and self-regulation.

1. Verbal Encouragement:

Offering verbal praise and encouragement for desired behaviors can be a powerful positive reinforcement technique for boys with ADHD. Expressing appreciation for their efforts, progress, and achievements can boost their self-confidence, reinforce positive behaviors, and motivate continued success.

2. Reward Systems:

Implementing a reward system that offers incentives for completing tasks, following instructions, and demonstrating positive behaviors can be an effective positive reinforcement strategy for boys with ADHD. Using tokens, stickers, or points that can be exchanged for rewards can help reinforce desired behaviors and provide a visual incentive for progress.

3. Breaks and Movement:

Allowing boys with ADHD to take short breaks and engage in physical movement activities can serve as positive reinforcement for their focus and self-regulation. Incorporating opportunities for movement breaks, sensory activities, or outdoor play can help them release excess energy, improve concentration, and enhance their overall well-being.

4. Structured Routine:
Creating a structured routine with clear expectations, schedules, and transitions can be a valuable positive reinforcement technique for boys with ADHD. Consistent routines help establish predictability, reduce anxiety, and reinforce positive behaviors by providing a sense of structure and organization.

5. Social Rewards:
Utilizing social rewards, such as verbal praise, high-fives, or quality time with caregivers, can serve as positive reinforcement for boys with ADHD. Positive social interactions, gestures of affection, and expressions of approval can help strengthen their self-esteem, build positive relationships, and foster a sense of connection and support.

6. Goal Setting and Progress Tracking:
Setting achievable goals and tracking progress can be an effective positive reinforcement technique for boys with ADHD. Breaking tasks into small, manageable steps, celebrating milestones, and acknowledging achievements along the way can reinforce their efforts, build resilience, and promote a sense of accomplishment.

7. Immediate Feedback:
Providing immediate feedback and reinforcement for positive behaviors enables boys with ADHD to make direct connections between their actions and the outcomes. Prompt acknowledgment, praise, or rewards following desired behaviors helps reinforce positive habits, enhance motivation, and encourage continued engagement in those behaviors.

8. Visual Supports:
Using visual supports, such as charts, checklists, or pictorial schedules, can help boys with

ADHD understand expectations, track progress, and reinforce positive behaviors. Visual aids provide a clear and concrete way to communicate goals, tasks, and rewards, facilitating comprehension and motivation.

9. Consistency and Predictability:
Consistency and predictability are essential aspects of positive reinforcement for boys with ADHD. Maintaining a consistent reinforcement system, establishing clear expectations, and delivering rewards predictably help create a stable and supportive environment that fosters positive behaviors, reinforces self-regulation, and enhances motivation.

preparing your child for the world by developing social awareness

Preparing a child with ADHD for the world involves developing social awareness, communication skills, and emotional intelligence to navigate relationships, work collaboratively, and interact effectively with others. While ADHD can present challenges in social settings, implementing strategies to enhance social awareness and skills can empower children to build positive connections, foster empathy, and thrive in diverse social environments.

1. Building Empathy and Perspective-Taking:
Encouraging children with ADHD to develop empathy and perspective-taking skills can enhance their social awareness and understanding of others' feelings, thoughts, and experiences. Teaching empathy through storytelling, role-playing, and reflective discussions can help children recognize emotions, show compassion, and build meaningful connections with others.

2. Improving Social Communication:
Enhancing social communication skills, such as active listening, clear articulation, and reciprocal conversation, is essential for children with ADHD to engage effectively in social interactions. Teaching strategies for initiating

conversations, maintaining eye contact, and responding appropriately can bolster social confidence and build rapport with peers and adults.

3. Practicing Social Problem-Solving:
Practicing social problem-solving techniques allows children with ADHD to navigate social challenges,resolve conflicts, and make informed decisions in social situations. Encouraging children to identify problems, consider alternative solutions, and evaluate outcomes fosters critical thinking, flexibility, and effective decision-making skills in social contexts.

4. Promoting Social Flexibility and Adaptability:
Promoting social flexibility involves helping children with ADHD adapt to changing social environments, navigate social cues, and adjust to new expectations. Encouraging flexibility, open-mindedness, and willingness to compromise can enhance children's social resilience, broaden their perspectives, and

strengthen their ability to interact with diverse individuals.

5. Enhancing Social Interaction Skills:
Developing social interaction skills, such as sharing, taking turns, showing appreciation, and respecting boundaries, is crucial for children with ADHD to engage positively in social settings. Providing opportunities for cooperative activities, group projects, and collaborative play can foster teamwork, cooperation, and mutual respect among peers.

6. Building Self-Regulation and Emotional Awareness:
Building self-regulation and emotional awareness empowers children with ADHD to manage their emotions, control impulses, and respond appropriately in social situations. Teaching techniques for self-calming, self-monitoring, and emotion regulation supports children in recognizing and expressing emotions, enhancing self-control and social competence.

7. Encouraging Social Play and Positive Relationships:

Encouraging social play and fostering positive relationships can help children with ADHD develop social skills, build friendships, and experience a sense of belonging. Providing opportunities for structured playdates, group activities, and social clubs promotes social engagement, communication, and camaraderie, nurturing social connections and peer support.

8. Supporting Social Learning and Reinforcement:

Supporting social learning through modeling, coaching, and reinforcement can help children with ADHD internalize social norms, practice social skills, and apply learned strategies in real-life situations. Providing feedback, positive reinforcement, and consistent guidance encourages children to generalize social skills, adapt to diverse social settings, and thrive in social interactions.

Chapter 5: Parenting Tips

Parenting is a rewarding journey filled with challenges, triumphs, and growth for both children and parents. For parents navigating the joys and complexities of raising children, especially those with Attention-Deficit/Hyperactivity Disorder (ADHD), a thoughtful approach, effective communication, and supportive strategies can make a significant difference in fostering positive relationships, promoting well-being, and empowering children to thrive.

1. Establish Consistent Routine:
Creating a consistent routine with predictable schedules, structured activities, and clear expectations can help children with ADHD feel organized, secure, and prepared for daily tasks and transitions. Establishing routines for waking up, meals, homework, playtime, and bedtime

provides stability, reduces stress, and supports focus and self-regulation.

2. Practice Positive Reinforcement:
Using positive reinforcement techniques, such as verbal praise, rewards, and encouragement, to acknowledge and reinforce desired behaviors can motivate children with ADHD to exhibit positive actions, stay engaged in tasks, and build self-esteem. Celebrating achievements, efforts, and progress fosters confidence, resilience, and intrinsic motivation.

3. Foster Effective Communication:
Promoting open, honest, and constructive communication with children involves active listening, empathy, and validation of their thoughts, feelings, and experiences. Encouraging children with ADHD to express themselves, ask questions, and share concerns creates a supportive, nurturing environment and strengthens the parent-child bond.

4. Set Clear Expectations and Limits:
Establishing clear, age-appropriate expectations, boundaries, and rules helps children with ADHD understand guidelines, responsibilities, and consequences. Consistent enforcement of limits with logical consequences, praise for compliance, and constructive feedback for misbehavior fosters accountability, self-discipline, and respect for rules.

5. Encourage Independence and Decision-Making:
Empowering children with ADHD to make choices, solve problems, and take ownership of tasks promotes independence, self-confidence, and self-efficacy. Providing opportunities for decision-making, offering guidance, and celebrating autonomy nurtures responsibility, critical thinking skills, and initiative in children.

6. Practice Patience and Flexibility:
Parenting children with ADHD requires patience, understanding, and flexibility in navigating challenges, setbacks, and unexpected

situations. Cultivating a calm, compassionate demeanor, adapting to changing circumstances, and maintaining a positive attitude model resilience, adaptability, and emotional regulation for children.

7. Collaborate with Educators and Healthcare Providers:

Building collaborative partnerships with teachers, school counselors, and healthcare professionals can enhance support, communication , and continuity of care for children with ADHD. Sharing information, collaborating on interventions, and aligning strategies between home and school settings can optimize academic success, social-emotional well-being, and comprehensive treatment for children.

8. Self-Care for Parents:

Prioritizing self-care, well-being, and balance is essential for parents caring for children with ADHD. Taking time for rest, relaxation, and personal interests, seeking support from friends, family, or support groups, and practicing self-compassion and self-care rituals promote resilience, emotional health, and effective parenting.

9. Seek Professional Guidance and Resources: Accessing professional guidance, resources, and support services from mental health professionals, ADHD specialists, and parenting workshops can provide valuable insights, strategies, and tools for managing ADHD-related challenges, enhancing parenting skills, and fostering a nurturing, proactive environment for children.

Overstimulation

Overstimulation is a common challenge experienced by individuals with (ADHD), often leading to difficulties in focus, attention, and emotional regulation. Overstimulation occurs when there is an excessive or overwhelming amount of sensory input, such as noise, light, or environmental stimuli, that can trigger feelings of overload or agitation in individuals with ADHD.

1. Sensory Sensitivity:
Individuals with ADHD may exhibit heightened sensitivity to sensory stimuli, such as loud noises, bright lights, strong scents, or crowded spaces. Sensory overload can overwhelm their nervous system, leading to feelings of stress, irritability, and discomfort. Managing sensory sensitivity is essential in reducing overstimulation and promoting a calmer environment for boys with ADHD.

2. Emotional Reactivity:
Overstimulation can trigger intense emotional reactions in individuals with ADHD, such as anxiety, frustration, or meltdowns. The combination of external stimuli and internal reactions can exacerbate emotional reactivity, making it challenging to regulate emotions and respond calmly to stressors. Developing emotional regulation strategies is crucial in

managing overstimulation and promoting emotional well-being.

3. Attention Difficulties:
Overstimulation can impair attention and focus in individuals with ADHD, hindering their ability to concentrate, process information, and complete tasks. Excessive sensory input can disrupt cognitive functioning, leading to distractibility, impulsivity, and decreased productivity. Implementing strategies to reduce environmental distractions and promote sustained attention can help mitigate attention difficulties associated with overstimulation.

4. Behavior Changes:
Overstimulation can manifest in behavioral changes, such as restlessness, agitation, or withdrawal, in individuals with ADHD. Heightened sensory input can cause discomfort and disorientation, prompting behavioral responses that may include avoidance, aggression, or shutdown. Recognizing and addressing behavior changes resulting from

overstimulation is essential in providing support and managing challenges effectively.

5. Cognitive Overload:

Experiencing sensory overload can overwhelm cognitive resources in individuals with ADHD, leading to cognitive overload and difficulty processing information. Cognitive tasks, such as decision-making, problem-solving, and organizing thoughts, can become taxing when the brain is inundated with excessive stimuli. Implementing strategies to reduce cognitive demands and promote cognitive efficiency can help alleviate cognitive overload associated with overstimulation.

6. Fatigue and Exhaustion:

Prolonged exposure to overstimulation can deplete energy reserves and lead to mental and physical fatigue in individuals with ADHD. Coping with sensory overload, emotional reactivity, attention difficulties, and behavior changes can be draining, contributing to feelings of exhaustion and burnout. Self-care practices, such as rest, relaxation, and stress management, are essential in combating fatigue and promoting overall well-being.

7. Strategies for Managing Overstimulation:
Developing strategies to manage overstimulation is key in supporting individuals with ADHD in navigating sensory challenges and promoting self-regulation. Creating a calming environment, establishing routines, using sensory tools (such as noise-canceling headphones or fidget toys), practicing mindfulness, and engaging in relaxation techniques can help regulate sensory input, reduce emotional reactivity, and enhance coping mechanisms in response to overstimulation.

8. Support and Understanding:
Providing support, validation, and understanding for individuals experiencing overstimulation is crucial in promoting a safe and inclusive environment for individuals with ADHD. Recognizing the impact of overstimulation on attention, emotions, and behavior, offering

reassurance and accommodations, and fostering open communication can create a supportive atmosphere that empowers individuals with ADHD to manage overstimulation effectively and thrive in their daily lives.

Help your kid son relieve emotional tension

Navigating the emotional challenges that can accompany Attention-Deficit/Hyperactivity Disorder (ADHD) requires compassion, understanding, and proactive strategies to support your son in managing emotional tension and promoting emotional well-being. By creating a nurturing and empathetic environment, implementing tools for emotional regulation, and fostering open communication, parents can help their sons navigate emotional tension and develop healthy coping skills.

1. Encourage Open Communication:
Create a safe and supportive space for your son to express his feelings, thoughts, and concerns openly. Encouraging open communication enables him to share his emotions, experiences, and challenges, fostering trust, connection, and emotional expression. Actively listen, validate his feelings, and offer non-judgmental support to promote emotional well-being and self-awareness.

2. Teach Emotional Regulation Techniques:
Help your son develop effective emotional regulation techniques to manage intense feelings, calm anxiety, and navigate emotional tension. Techniques such as deep breathing exercises, mindfulness practices, progressive muscle relaxation, and guided imagery can promote relaxation, reduce stress, and enhance self-control during emotional moments.

3. Promote Physical Activity and Movement:
Encouraging physical activity and movement can help your son release pent-up energy, reduce

emotional tension, and improve mood regulation. Engaging in regular exercise, outdoor play, or sports activities can promote relaxation, boost endorphins, and support emotional well-being, providing a healthy outlet for emotional expression and stress relief.

4. Establish Structured Routines:
Creating structured routines and predictable schedules can help your son feel secure, organized, and in control, reducing emotional tension and promoting stability. Consistent routines for daily activities, bedtime, meals, and homework can provide a sense of predictability, reduce anxiety, and enhance emotional regulation by fostering a stable and supportive environment.

5. Practice Mindfulness and Grounding Techniques:
Introduce mindfulness and grounding techniques to help your son stay present, center his thoughts, and manage emotional tension. Mindfulness practices, such as focused

breathing, body scans, and sensory awareness exercises, can promote emotional balance, reduce impulsivity, and cultivate self-awareness in moments of heightened stress or tension.

6. Offer Comfort and Support:
Provide comfort, reassurance, and emotional support to your son during times of emotional distress or tension. Comforting gestures, hugs, and words of encouragement can convey empathy, caring, and understanding, validating his emotions,feelings, and experiences. Offering a listening ear, a comforting presence, and a safe space for emotional expression can help your son feel understood, valued, and supported, enhancing emotional well-being and resilience.

7. Set Realistic Expectations:
Establishing realistic expectations and setting achievable goals can help your son manage emotional tension and reduce feelings of pressure or overwhelm. Encourage a growth mindset, celebrate small victories, and acknowledge effort over perfection to foster a

positive self-image, boost confidence, and alleviate emotional stress associated with high expectations.

8. Seek Professional Support:
If your son experiences persistent emotional tension, struggles with mood regulation, or exhibits signs of distress, consider seeking professional support from a counselor, therapist, or mental health professional. Professional guidance, therapy, or behavioral interventions can provide additional tools, resources, and strategies to help your son effectively manage emotional challenges associated with ADHD and promote overall emotional well-being.

Chapter 6: School Success Strategies

Understanding ADHD in the School Setting:
ADHD, or Attention-Deficit/Hyperactivity Disorder, is a neurodevelopmental condition that can impact a child's ability to focus, organize, and regulate their behavior. In a school setting, boys with ADHD may struggle with staying attentive, following instructions, completing tasks, and managing their impulses.

Creating a Supportive Environment:
One key aspect of helping boys with ADHD succeed in school is creating a supportive environment that caters to their unique needs. This includes establishing clear routines, providing visual aids, minimizing distractions, and offering regular breaks to help them stay focused and engaged.

Effective Communication:
Effective communication between teachers, parents, and the child with ADHD is essential for academic success. Teachers should openly communicate with parents about the child's progress, challenges, and strategies that work well. Encouraging open communication can help create a collaborative and supportive school environment.

Individualized Education Plans (IEPs):
Individualized Education Plans (IEPs) and 504 Plans:
For boys with ADHD, having an Individualized Education Plan (IEP) or a 504 Plan can provide tailored support and accommodations to help them succeed in school. These plans outline specific strategies, accommodations, and services that address the child's unique needs and ensure equal access to education.

Teaching Strategies:
Teachers play a crucial role in supporting boys with ADHD in the classroom. Using interactive

and hands-on teaching methods, breaking down tasks into smaller steps, providing clear instructions, and offering positive reinforcement can all help boys with ADHD stay engaged and focused.

Behavior Management:
Managing behavior in the classroom is important for creating a conducive learning environment for boys with ADHD. Implementing positive behavior management strategies, such as praise, rewards, and consequences, can help boys with ADHD understand expectations and regulate their behavior effectively.

Building Self-Esteem and Confidence:
Boys with ADHD may face challenges that impact their self-esteem and confidence in school. Encouraging their strengths, providing opportunities for success, and offering supportive feedback can help build their self-esteem and foster a positive attitude towards learning.

Parental Involvement and Support:
Parents play a vital role in supporting their child with ADHD in the school setting. Communicating regularly with teachers , attending school meetings, and staying involved in their child's education can help parents understand their child's needs and advocate for appropriate support and accommodations.

Collaboration and Support Services:
Collaboration among teachers, parents, school administrators, and support services can enhance the overall support for boys with ADHD in school. Utilizing resources such as school psychologists, counselors, and special education services can provide additional support and guidance for addressing the unique needs of boys with ADHD.

Managing ADHD Symptoms in School

Within the classroom, children with ADHD often possess remarkable creativity and energy, but may encounter challenges when it comes to focusing, organizing tasks, and controlling impulses. By implementing targeted strategies, educators can empower these students to thrive academically and harness their full potential.

Embracing Individuality:
Recognizing that each child with ADHD is unique in their strengths and challenges is paramount. By acknowledging and celebrating the diverse qualities of these students, educators can create an inclusive environment that fosters growth, resilience, and success.

Building a Supportive Framework:
Establishing a structured and supportive framework within the school setting is essential for children with ADHD. By providing clear instructions, implementing visual aids, and structuring tasks into manageable steps, educators can promote organization, productivity, and engagement.

Nurturing Focus and Attention:
Helping children with ADHD maintain focus and attention in the classroom requires innovative approaches. Introducing movement breaks, incorporating interactive learning activities, and offering flexible seating arrangements can stimulate engagement, reduce restlessness, and enhance learning outcomes.

Empowering Self-Regulation:
Equipping students with ADHD with self-regulation skills empowers them to proactively manage their symptoms and navigate challenges independently. By teaching mindfulness techniques, promoting

self-monitoring strategies, and fostering self-advocacy, educators can cultivate a sense of ownership and autonomy in these students.

Cultivating Positive Reinforcement:
Harnessing the power of positive reinforcement can inspire motivation, boost self-esteem, and reinforce desired behaviors in children with ADHD. By providing praise, rewards, and encouragement for efforts and achievements, educators can create a positive and supportive learning environment that nurtures growth and development.

Fostering Collaboration and Communication:
Collaboration among teachers, parents, and support services is key to effectively managing ADHD symptoms in school. By promoting open communication, sharing insights, and developing personalized plans that cater to the unique needs of each child, educators can create a holistic support network that enhances academic success.

Collaborating with Teachers for Academic Support

This page will explore the importance of building strong partnerships between parents, caregivers, and teachers to enhance the educational experience of kids with this disorder

Understanding the Role of Teachers:
Teachers play a vital role in the academic success of students. They are responsible for creating a supportive learning environment, delivering instruction, assessing student progress, and providing individualized support to meet the diverse needs of students in the classroom.

Establishing Open Communication:
Open communication is key to effective collaboration between parents, caregivers, and teachers. Regular communication channels, such as emails, phone calls, or meetings, can facilitate

the exchange of information about a student's progress, challenges, and academic needs.

Sharing Information and Insights:
Parents and caregivers can provide valuable insights about their child's strengths, challenges, preferences, and learning styles to teachers. By sharing information about their child's interests, motivations, and educational goals, parents can help teachers tailor instruction to meet the unique needs of the student.

Setting Academic Goals:
Collaborating with teachers to set academic goals that are specific, measurable, achievable, relevant, and time-bound (SMART) can guide the educational journey of students. By working together to establish clear objectives, parents, caregivers, and teachers can monitor progress, track achievements, and support student growth and development.

Implementing Support Strategies:
Teachers can implement a range of support strategies to address the individual needs of students. This may include differentiated instruction, accommodations, modifications, specialized interventions, and extra support services to help students overcome challenges and reach their full academic potential.

Participating in Parent-Teacher Meetings:
Attending parent-teacher meetings, such as parent-teacher conferences or Individualized Education Program (IEP) meetings, provides an opportunity for parents, caregivers, and teachers to discuss student progress, share concerns, celebrate achievements, and collaborate on strategies to support the student's academic success.

Providing Consistent Support:
Consistent support and encouragement from both teachers and parents are essential for motivating students, fostering a positive attitude towards learning, and promoting academic

growth. By working together as a team, parents and teachers can create a supportive and nurturing environment that empowers students to thrive academically.

Chapter 7: Nurturing communal Relationships

Communal relationships are characterized by shared values, trust, and a sense of belonging among community members. These connections go beyond mere acquaintanceships and create a supportive network where individuals feel supported, understood, and valued.

Creating a Sense of Belonging:
A key aspect of communal relationships is creating a sense of belonging for all members of the community. This involves promoting inclusivity, celebrating diversity, and offering support to individuals from all backgrounds to foster a welcoming and accepting environment.

Building Trust and Mutual Respect:
Trust and mutual respect form the foundation of strong communal relationships. By communicating openly, listening attentively, honoring commitments, and showing empathy towards others, community members can build trust and strengthen their connections with one another.

Encouraging Collaboration and Cooperation:
Collaboration and cooperation are essential in nurturing communal relationships. By working together towards common goals, sharing resources, and supporting one another's endeavors, community members can foster a spirit of cooperation that benefits everyone in the community and promotes a sense of unity and collective achievement.

Promoting Positive Communication:
Positive communication is key to nurturing communal relationships. By practicing active listening, offering constructive feedback,

expressing gratitude, and resolving conflicts peacefully, individuals can foster clear, respectful, and empathetic communication that builds stronger connections within the community.

Supporting Each Other:
Supporting one another is a cornerstone of communal relationships. By offering help, encouragement, and emotional support to fellow community members during times of need, individuals can create a culture of care, compassion, and solidarity that strengthens the communal bond.

Celebrating Successes and Milestones:
Celebrating successes and milestones within the community fosters a sense of achievement and pride among its members. By recognizing and acknowledging the accomplishments of individuals, groups, or the community as a whole, community members can inspire positivity, motivation, and a shared sense of progress.

Embracing Diversity and Inclusion:
Embracing diversity and inclusion enriches communal relationships by appreciating, respecting, and celebrating the differences among community members. By creating an inclusive environment that values diverse perspectives, backgrounds, and experiences, individuals can foster a sense of unity and understanding within the community.

Telling your super boy how great his future looks

Encouraging and supporting your super boy with ADHD can make a significant difference in shaping his future. This section explores how to convey positivity, optimism, and belief in his potential, regardless of any challenges posed by the disorder.

Recognizing Your Super Boy's Strengths:
Every child, including your super boy, possesses unique strengths, talents, and qualities that define who they are. By recognizing and celebrating his strengths, such as creativity, resilience, and determination, you can instill a sense of confidence and self-worth in him.

Fostering a Growth Mindset:
Encouraging a growth mindset in your superboy involves nurturing his belief that abilities can be developed through effort, perseverance, and learning from setbacks. By framing challenges as opportunities for growth and encouraging a positive attitude towards learning and self-improvement, you can empower him to face obstacles with resilience and determination.

Setting High Expectations:
Setting high expectations for your super boy communicates your belief in his capabilities and potential. By challenging him to reach for his goals, pursue his passions, and strive for excellence in all that he does, you can inspire

him to dream big and work towards a bright future, irrespective of any challenges presented by ADHD.

Emphasizing Effort and Progress:
Rather than focusing solely on outcomes, emphasize the importance of effort, progress, and perseverance in your super boy's journey. Acknowledge and celebrate his hard work, determination, and incremental improvements, reinforcing the idea that growth and success are the result of continuous effort and dedication.

Providing Encouragement and Support:
Offering consistent encouragement, support, and reassurance to your super boy can boost his confidence, motivation, and sense of self-belief. Be his cheerleader, provide words of affirmation, and offer a listening ear during moments of doubt or difficulty, showing him that you believe in his abilities and potential.

Encouraging Independence and Self-Advocacy:
Empowering your super boy to advocate for himself, express his needs and preferences, and take ownership of his education and well-being instills a sense of independence and self-reliance. Encourage him to voice his thoughts, ask for accommodations when needed, and actively participate in decision-making processes, fostering a sense of agency and empowerment.

Creating a Vision for the Future:
Help your superboy envision his future by exploring his interests, passions, and goals. Encourage him to dream big, set aspirations, and plan steps towards achieving his vision, while emphasizing that ADHD does not define his potential or limit his future possibilities.

Celebrating Achievements and Milestones:
Celebrate your super boy's achievements, no matter how big or small, to acknowledge his progress, hard work, and dedication. By recognizing his accomplishments, you reinforce

his sense of accomplishment, boost his self-esteem, and motivate him to continue striving towards his goals with determination and optimism.

Resolving Conflict with your little boy

Resolving conflicts with a child who has ADHD requires patience, understanding, and tailored strategies to address their unique needs. This section explores practical and effective ways to navigate conflict situations with your little boy with ADHD in clear and simple language.

Understanding ADHD and Conflict:
ADHD can impact a child's behavior, emotions, and interactions, making conflict resolution more challenging. It's important to recognize that impulsive behavior, inattention, and emotional dysregulation may contribute to conflicts. Understanding how ADHD influences

your child's responses can guide your approach to resolving conflicts.

Maintaining Calm and Positive Communication: When conflicts arise, staying calm and using positive language is essential. Speak to your little boy in a calm tone, focusing on specific behaviors rather than making general criticisms. Encourage open communication and active listening to validate his feelings and perspectives.

Setting Clear Expectations: Establishing clear expectations and boundaries can help prevent conflicts and guide behavior. Clearly communicate rules, routines, and consequences to your little boy with ADHD in a straightforward and consistent manner. Provide visual cues, such as charts or schedules, to reinforce expectations effectively.

Using Visual Tools and Structure: Visual tools and structured routines can support your child with ADHD in understanding expectations and managing conflicts. Visual aids such as behavior charts, checklists, or visual schedules can help him stay organized, follow routines, and understand the steps involved in conflict resolution.

Teaching Problem-Solving Skills:
Encourage your little boy with ADHD to develop problem-solving skills to address conflicts effectively. Teach him simple steps to identify the issue, brainstorm solutions, evaluate options, and choose a resolution. Practicing problem-solving can empower him to navigate conflicts independently.

Offering Positive Reinforcement:
Positive reinforcement is a powerful tool in shaping behavior and resolving conflicts. Praise your little boy for using appropriate conflict resolution strategies, exhibiting patience, or showing empathy towards others. Positive feedback and rewards can motivate him to repeat positive behaviors.

Implementing Breaks and Self-Regulation Techniques:

During heated conflicts, provide opportunities for your little boy to take breaks and engage in self-regulation techniques. Encourage deep breathing exercises, mindfulness practices, or physical activities to help him calm down and refocus before addressing the conflict.

Collaborating with Professionals:

If conflicts persist or become challenging to manage, seek guidance from mental health professionals, counselors, or educators experienced in working with children with ADHD. Collaborating with experts can provide additional strategies, resources, and support tailored to your child's unique needs and challenges related to ADHD.

Encouraging Empathy and Understanding:

Promote empathy in your interactions with your little boy with ADHD and encourage him to consider the feelings of others during conflicts. Help him understand the impact of his actions on others and encourage him to express empathy and compassion towards those involved in the conflict.

Celebrating Progress and Efforts:
Acknowledge and celebrate the progress, efforts, and improvements your little boy makes in conflict resolution. Recognize his attempts to apply strategies, remain calm, and communicate effectively during conflicts. Celebrating even small steps forward can reinforce positive behaviors and motivate further growth.

Chapter 8: Self-Care for Parents

Parenting a child with ADHD can be rewarding yet challenging, requiring patience, understanding, and self-care. This page talks about practical strategies to help parents maintain their well-being while supporting their children with ADHD in clear and simple language.

Understanding the Importance of Self-Care:
Self-care is essential for parents raising children with ADHD to prevent burnout, manage stress, and maintain their physical, emotional, and mental well-being. Taking time to care for yourself enables you to be a more effective and resilient caregiver for your child.

Prioritizing Rest and Sleep:
Getting adequate rest and quality sleep is crucial for parents' overall health and well-being. Establish a consistent bedtime routine, prioritize restful sleep, and create a relaxing sleep environment to improve sleep quality and restore energy levels.

Setting Realistic Expectations:
Avoid placing unrealistic expectations on yourself as a parent. Recognize that parenting a child with ADHD presents unique challenges, and it's okay to seek support, ask for help, and practice self-compassion.

Seeking Support and Community:
Connecting with other parents, support groups, or mental health professionals can provide invaluable support and understanding during challenging times. Joining a support group for parents of children with ADHD, attending counseling sessions, or seeking guidance from a therapist can offer emotional support, practical advice, and coping strategies.

Engaging in Stress-Relief Activities:
Incorporating stress-relief activities into your daily routine can help alleviate anxiety and promote relaxation. Practice mindfulness meditation, deep breathing exercises, yoga, or engage in physical activities such as walking, jogging, or gardening to reduce stress and promote mental clarity.

Taking Breaks and Time for Yourself:
It's important to carve out time for self-care and personal activities to recharge and rejuvenate. Schedule regular breaks for self-care, whether it's reading a book, taking a bath, enjoying a hobby, or simply relaxing alone. Prioritizing "me time" is essential for refueling your energy and resilience.

Balancing Responsibilities:
Finding a balance between caregiving responsibilities, work, household chores, and self-care is key to managing stress and preventing burnout. Delegate tasks, establish

boundaries, and prioritize activities that bring you joy and relaxation to maintain a healthy work-life balance.

Practicing Self-Compassion:
Be kind and compassionate towards yourself as a parent. Acknowledge your efforts, embrace imperfections, and practice self-compassion in moments of self-doubt or overwhelm. Treat yourself with the same understanding and empathy you extend to your child, recognizing that self-care is a necessary component of effective caregiving.

Nurturing Positive Relationships:
Maintaining healthy relationships with your partner, family members, and friends can provide emotional support and companionship during challenging times. Communicate openly, seek guidance from loved ones, and nurture positive connections to foster a sense of belonging and community.

Importance of Self-Care for Parents of Children with ADHD

Self-care involves prioritizing your physical, emotional, and mental well-being to ensure you have the resilience and capacity to meet the needs of your child with ADHD. By taking care of yourself, you enhance your ability to provide the necessary support, patience, and understanding required in parenting a boy with ADHD.

Building Resilience and Stress Management:
Parenting a child with ADHD can bring unique challenges and stressors. Engaging in self-care practices such as exercise, mindfulness, relaxation techniques, and seeking support can help you build resilience, manage stress effectively, and cope with the demands of caregiving.

Prioritizing Mental Health:
Maintaining good mental health is crucial for parents of children with ADHD. Taking time for self-reflection, seeking counseling or therapy, practicing self-compassion, and ensuring regular breaks can support your mental well-being and enhance your ability to navigate the emotional ups and downs that may accompany raising a child with ADHD.

Physical Well-Being and Self-Care:
Caring for your physical health is an important aspect of self-care. Eating nutritious foods, staying active, getting adequate rest, and attending to your own health needs are essential for sustaining your energy levels, promoting overall well-being, and managing the demands of parenting a child with ADHD.

Setting Boundaries and Seeking Support:
Establishing boundaries around your time, responsibilities, and personal needs is key to preventing burnout and maintaining a healthy work-life balance. Seek support from friends,

family members, support groups, or mental health professionals to share your experiences, seek guidance, and receive emotional support when needed.

Engaging in Activities That Bring Joy:
Incorporating activities that bring joy, relaxation, and fulfillment into your daily routine is essential for self-care. Whether it's pursuing a hobby, spending time outdoors, engaging in creative outlets, or practicing mindfulness, making time for activities that nourish your spirit and bring you happiness is vital for your well-being.

Taking Breaks and Practicing Mindfulness:
Prioritizing breaks throughout your day, even in short intervals, can help you recharge, refocus, and reduce stress. Practicing mindfulness techniques such as deep breathing, meditation, or grounding exercises can help you stay present, calm your mind, and manage overwhelming emotions during challenging moments.

Promoting Positive Parenting:
By practicing self-care, you model healthy behaviors and coping strategies for your child with ADHD. Your self-care efforts can contribute to a positive, nurturing environment that fosters resilience, understanding, and emotional well-being for both you and your child.

Strategies for Stress Management and Burnout Prevention

Stress and burnout are common challenges in today's fast-paced world, impacting physical, emotional, and mental well-being. This section explores practical strategies to manage stress effectively and prevent burnout, promoting overall health and resilience.

Understanding Stress and Burnout:
Stress is a natural response to perceived threats or demands, while burnout is a state of emotional, physical, and mental exhaustion caused by prolonged stress. Recognizing the signs of stress and burnout is the first step in addressing these challenges and prioritizing self-care.

Practice Mindfulness and Relaxation Techniques:
Engaging in mindfulness practices, such as deep breathing, meditation, or progressive muscle relaxation, can help reduce stress levels, promote relaxation, and enhance mental clarity. Taking short breaks throughout the day to practice relaxation techniques can foster a sense of calm and focus.

Establish Healthy Boundaries:
Setting boundaries around work responsibilities, personal time, and commitments is vital for preventing burnout. Learn to say no to excessive demands, prioritize your tasks effectively, and

allocate time for self-care activities that replenish your energy and well-being. Respecting your boundaries helps maintain a healthy work-life balance and prevent overwhelm.

Regular Physical Activity:
Incorporating regular physical activity into your routine is an effective way to manage stress and improve overall well-being. Exercise releases endorphins, the body's natural stress relievers, and promotes physical health. Choose activities you enjoy, whether it's walking, jogging, yoga, or dancing, and make time for movement each day.

Healthy Eating Habits:
Nutritious foods that nourish your body and mind play a key role in stress management and overall health. Make eating a well-balanced diet high on whole grains, fruits, vegetables, lean meats, and healthy fats a priority. Steer clear of processed foods, sugar, and caffeine excess as these can exacerbate anxiety and mood swings.

Seek Social Support:

Building a strong support network of friends, family members, or peers can provide emotional support and companionship during times of stress. Reach out to loved ones for connection, conversation, and encouragement. Sharing your feelings and experiences with trusted individuals can offer perspective and reduce feelings of isolation.

Practice Time Management:

Effective time management strategies can help you prioritize tasks, set realistic goals, and reduce feelings of overwhelm. Use tools such as to-do lists, calendars, and schedules to organize your day, delegate tasks when possible,and break larger projects into manageable steps. By managing your time efficiently, you can increase productivity, reduce stress, and prevent burnout.

Embrace Self-Care Activities:

Incorporating self-care activities that bring you joy, relaxation, and fulfillment is essential for maintaining your well-being and preventing burnout. Engage in activities that recharge your energy, such as reading, listening to music, spending time in nature, pursuing hobbies, or taking a soothing bath. Prioritize self-care as a regular part of your routine to nurture your mind, body, and spirit.

Seek Professional Help:
If stress and burnout persist despite self-care efforts, don't hesitate to seek help from a mental health professional, counselor, or therapist. Professional support can provide guidance, tools, and coping strategies tailored to your individual needs, helping you address underlying stressors and develop effective ways to manage stress and prevent burnout.

Chapter 9: Building Resilience in Children with ADHD

The capacity to overcome obstacles, failures, and adversity is resilience. For children with ADHD, developing resilience is crucial for managing difficulties, building confidence, and navigating the complexities of the condition. This section explores practical strategies to help foster resilience in children with ADHD in a clear and simple manner.

Encouraging Positive Self-Image:
Promoting a positive self-image in children with ADHD is essential for building resilience. Encourage them to recognize and celebrate their strengths, talents, and unique qualities. Emphasize that having ADHD does not define their worth or potential, and that they are capable of achieving success in various areas of their lives.

Developing Coping Strategies:
Help children with ADHD develop coping strategies to manage challenges and regulate their emotions. Teach them relaxation techniques, such as deep breathing or mindfulness exercises, to help them calm their minds and bodies during stressful situations. Encourage problem-solving skills and positive thinking patterns to foster resilience in the face of difficulties.

Supporting Self-Advocacy:
Empower children with ADHD to advocate for their needs, preferences, and accommodations. Teach them to communicate assertively, express their feelings, and seek help when necessary. By learning to self-advocate, children with ADHD can take an active role in shaping their experiences and accessing the support they require.

Building Social Skills:
Social skills are essential for children with ADHD to navigate interpersonal relationships

and peer interactions. Provide opportunities for socialization, role-play social scenarios, and teach effective communication strategies. Building strong social skills can enhance children's resilience by fostering positive relationships and connections with others.

Encouraging Growth Mindset:
Promote a growth mindset in children with ADHD by emphasizing the importance of effort, perseverance, and learning from mistakes. Teach them to view challenges as opportunities for growth and development rather than obstacles. Encourage a positive attitude towards learning, resilience, and self-improvement.

Setting Realistic Goals:
Help children with ADHD set realistic goals that are attainable and aligned with their abilities. Break down large goals into smaller achievable steps, celebrate progress and achievements, and provide positive reinforcement to motivate continued effort. By setting and accomplishing goals, children with ADHD can build

confidence, resilience, and a sense of accomplishment.

Fostering Independence:
Encourage independence and autonomy in children with ADHD by offering opportunities for them to make decisions, solve problems, and take responsibility for their actions. Support their efforts to try new things, learn from experiences, and develop a sense of self-reliance. Building independence can strengthen their resilience and self-confidence.

Building their intellectual positively

Developing a child's intellectual abilities positively is essential for fostering learning, critical thinking, and problem-solving skills.

Encouraging Curiosity and Exploration:
Fostering a sense of curiosity and exploration is fundamental to enhancing intellectual

development in boys. Encourage them to ask questions, seek answers, and engage in hands-on learning experiences that spark their curiosity and creativity.

Reading and Literacy Promotion:
Reading is a cornerstone of intellectual development and language skills. Encourage boys to read widely, explore different genres, and discover the joy of storytelling. Provide access to age-appropriate books, visit libraries, and engage in shared reading experiences to cultivate a love for literature and literacy.

Critical Thinking and Problem-Solving Skills:
Developing critical thinking and problem-solving skills equips boys with the ability to analyze information, make sound decisions, and solve complex problems. Encourage them to think critically, consider different perspectives, and approach challenges with creativity and perseverance.

STEM Education and Hands-On Learning:
Introducing boys to STEM (Science, Technology, Engineering, and Mathematics) education enhances their intellectual development through hands-on learning experiences. Students can engage in STEM activities, experiments, and projects that foster curiosity, innovation, and analytical thinking, promoting intellectual growth in various disciplines.

Creative Arts and Expression:
Encouraging boys to explore the creative arts, such as music, art, drama, and writing, nurtures their imagination, self-expression, and emotional intelligence. Engaging in artistic pursuits enhances cognitive skills, problem-solving abilities, and enhances intellectual development through creative expression.

Encouraging Independent Thinking:
Promote independent thinking in boys by allowing them to express their opinions, explore their interests, and engage in decision-making

processes. Encourage them to question assumptions, consider alternative viewpoints, and develop their unique perspectives through independent thought and reflection.

Supporting Continuous Learning:
Foster a culture of continuous learning and intellectual growth by exposing boys to diverse experiences, challenges, and opportunities for growth. Encourage participation in extracurricular activities, educational programs, and enrichment opportunities that expand their knowledge, skills, and intellectual abilities.

Embracing Technology and Innovation:
Integrating technology and fostering innovation can enhance boys' intellectual development in the digital age. Encourage them to explore technology, coding, digital tools, and innovation initiatives that promote creativity, problem-solving, and adaptability in a rapidly evolving world.

Encouraging Growth Mindset and Self-Image

A growth mindset is the belief that abilities can be developed through effort, perseverance, and learning from mistakes. Encouraging children to embrace a growth mindset fosters resilience, motivation, and a willingness to take on new challenges and learn from setbacks.

Promoting Effort and Persistence:
Encourage children to focus on their efforts, progress, and the process of learning rather than fixed outcomes or intelligence. Praising their hard work, perseverance, and willingness to tackle difficult tasks reinforces the importance of effort and resilience in achieving goals and overcoming obstacles.

Embracing Challenges and Learning Opportunities:
Teach children to embrace challenges as opportunities for growth and learning.

Encourage them to step out of their comfort zones, try new activities, and approach difficulties with a positive attitude. By viewing challenges as chances to learn and improve, children develop a sense of resilience and a passion for learning.

Celebrating Achievements and Progress:
Celebrate children's achievements, big or small, to acknowledge their efforts and accomplishments. Recognizing and celebrating milestones, progress, and successes boosts children's self-esteem, confidence, and motivation. Positive reinforcement and acknowledgment of their hard work reinforce a positive self-image and encourage continued growth.

Encouraging Positive Self-Talk:
Promote positive self-talk and self-affirmations in children to boost their self-image and confidence. Encourage them to replace negative self-talk with affirming, empowering statements that reinforce their strengths, abilities, and

worth. By fostering a positive inner dialogue, children develop a strong sense of self-worth and belief in their capabilities.

Modeling Growth Mindset Behaviors:
Lead by example and demonstrate a growth mindset in your own attitudes and behaviors. Show children that challenges, mistakes, and setbacks are opportunities for growth and learning. By modeling resilience, perseverance, and a positive outlook, you inspire children to adopt a similar mindset in their own lives.

Encouraging Risk-Taking and Innovation:
Encourage children to take risks, experiment, and think creatively in their pursuits. Provide opportunities for them to explore new ideas, try different approaches, and innovate in their activities. Embracing risk-taking and innovation fosters a growth mindset, resilience , and a sense of imagination in children, enabling them to see failures as stepping stones to success and creativity as a pathway to discovery.

Creating a Supportive Environment:
Establish a supportive and nurturing environment that validates children's efforts, encourages growth, and promotes self-expression. Provide constructive feedback, offer guidance, and create a safe space where children feel valued, respected, and empowered to explore their potential and embrace challenges.

Encouraging Perseverance and Resilience:
Teach children the importance of perseverance, resilience, and bouncing back from setbacks. Help them see failures as learning opportunities, setbacks as temporary obstacles, and challenges as stepping stones to growth. By fostering persistence and resilience, children develop the skills to overcome adversity and pursue their goals with determination.

Conclusion

As parents, caregivers, educators, and supporters of children with ADHD, it is essential to embrace a compassionate and understanding approach. By recognizing the strengths, talents, and resilience of these boys, we can nurture their potential, build their confidence, and foster a sense of belonging and acceptance.

Through the promotion of effective communication, positive reinforcement, tailored interventions, and a supportive environment, we can empower these children to thrive academically, emotionally, and socially. By encouraging a growth mindset, celebrating achievements, and fostering a positive self-image, we instill in them the belief that they can overcome challenges, learn from setbacks, and achieve their dreams.

As we navigate the complexities of ADHD, let us remember that every child is unique, every journey is valuable, and every small step forward is a triumph. Let us continue to advocate for understanding, acceptance, and support for children with ADHD, creating a world where their voices are heard, their strengths are celebrated,and their potential is limitless.

Remember, with patience, empathy, and a commitment to learning, we can help children with ADHD flourish and thrive. They are capable, they are valuable, and they are deserving of every opportunity to shine brightly in a world that embraces their differences and celebrates their strengths.

Glossary

- Key Terms and Definitions

1.   Attention-Deficit/Hyperactivity   Disorder (ADHD): A neurodevelopmental disorder characterized by a persistent pattern of inattention, hyperactivity, and impulsivity that can impact a child's daily functioning and overall well-being.

2. Resilience: The ability to bounce back from challenges, setbacks, and adversity, demonstrating adaptability, perseverance, and positive coping strategies in the face of difficulties.

3. Growth Mindset: The belief that abilities and intelligence can be developed through effort,

learning, and persistence, promoting a positive attitude towards challenges, learning, and personal growth.

4. Self-Image: The perception, beliefs, and feelings an individual holds about themselves, including self-esteem, self-worth, and self-perception that influence their confidence and self-concept.

5. Positive Reinforcement: A method of encouraging desired behaviors by providing rewards, praise, or positive feedback to reinforce and increase the likelihood of those behaviors occurring again in the future.

6. Mindfulness: The practice of focusing on the present moment with awareness and without judgment, cultivating mental clarity, emotional balance, and self-awareness.

7. Empathy: The ability to understand and share the feelings, perspectives, and experiences of others, demonstrating compassion,

understanding, and sensitivity towards the emotions and needs of others.

8. Self-Advocacy: The ability to assertively communicate one's thoughts, preferences, and needs in various situations, advocating for oneself and expressing personal rights and boundaries.

9. Critical Thinking: A cognitive skill that involves analyzing, evaluating, and synthesizing information to make reasoned judgments and decisions, promoting logical reasoning, problem-solving, and informed decision-making.

10. Social Skills: The communication, interaction, and relationship-building abilities that enable individuals to navigate social situations, establish connections, and engage effectively with others in various contexts.

11. Resilient Parenting: An approach to parenting that emphasizes nurturing resilience, adaptability, and coping skills in children,

fostering a supportive, encouraging, and growth-promoting environment.

12. Positive Self-Talk: The practice of using affirming, encouraging, and empowering language and thoughts to promote self-confidence, self-belief, and a constructive self-narrative that enhances self-esteem and mental well-being.

13. Well-Being: The state of being in good physical, emotional, and mental health, characterized by a sense of balance, fulfillment, and overall wellness in various aspects of one's life.

14. Supportive Environment: A setting that promotes a sense of safety,belonging, encouragement, and positive growth, providing a nurturing and empowering backdrop for personal development, learning, and well-being.

15. Growth and Development: The process of continuous physical, intellectual, emotional, and

social maturation and progress, encompassing learning, change, and improvement over time in various aspects of an individual's life.

16. Neurodevelopmental Disorder: A condition that affects the development of the nervous system, including the brain, impacting functions such as attention, behavior, and cognitive abilities in children with ADHD.

17. Social and Emotional Learning (SEL): The process of developing social-emotional skills such as self-awareness, self-management, social awareness, relationship skills, and responsible decision-making to enhance emotional intelligence and interpersonal relationships.

18. Executive Functioning: Cognitive processes that enable individuals to plan, organize, prioritize, manage time, focus attention, regulate behavior, and adapt to changing circumstances, crucial for academic and daily functioning in children with ADHD.

19. Coping Strategies: Adaptive techniques and behaviors used to manage stress, regulate emotions, and cope with challenges, promoting resilience, mental well-being, and effective problem-solving skills in children with ADHD.

20. Individualized Education Plan (IEP): A personalized education plan designed to address the specific academic, behavioral, and support needs of children with ADHD, outlining goals, accommodations, and services to optimize learning and development.

21. Behavioral Interventions: Strategies and techniques used to modify, reinforce, or change behaviors in children , including positive reinforcement, behavior modification, social skills training, and cognitive-behavioral approaches to promote positive behavioral outcomes and self-regulation in children with ADHD.

22. Emotional Regulation: The ability to recognize, understand, and manage one's

emotions effectively, including identifying triggers, coping with stress, and expressing feelings in a healthy and adaptive manner, essential for emotional well-being and social interactions in children with ADHD.

23. Neurodiversity: The concept that neurological differences, including ADHD, are a natural variation of the human brain rather than a disorder, promoting acceptance, appreciation, and inclusivity of diverse cognitive styles and abilities.

24. Multi-Modal Treatment: An approach that combines multiple interventions, such as medication, therapy, behavior management, and educational support, to address the complex needs of children with ADHD comprehensively and holistically.

25. Collaboration: The act of working together with parents, educators, healthcare providers, and support services to coordinate care, share information, and develop personalized strategies

and interventions to support the holistic well-being and academic success of children with ADHD.

26. Cognitive Flexibility: The ability to adapt and shift thinking, problem-solving strategies, and approaches in response to changing demands or new information, promoting adaptive behavior and resilience in children with ADHD.

27. Self-Esteem: The overall subjective sense of personal worth, value, and confidence that individuals hold about themselves, influencing their self-perception, self-belief, and emotional well-being in children with ADHD.

28. Time Management: The practice of planning, organizing, and prioritizing tasks, activities, and responsibilities effectively to optimize productivity, achieve goals, and reduce stress in children with ADHD.

29. Sensory Processing: The neurological process of receiving, interpreting, and responding to sensory information from the environment, such as touch, sound, sight, taste, and smell, which can influence behavior and attention in children with ADHD.

30. Impulse Control: The ability to regulate and manage impulsive behaviors, thoughts, and reactions, demonstrating self-discipline, inhibition, and decision-making skills to improve self-control and social interactions in children with ADHD.

31. Parent Advocacy: The active involvement, support, and advocacy of parents in securing services, accommodations, and support for their child with ADHD, promoting access to educational resources, healthcare, and community services.

32. Emotional Intelligence: The capacity to acquire knowledge, apply reasoning, solve problems, and adapt to new situations,

encompassing various cognitive abilities such as language, memory, spatial awareness, and critical thinking in children with ADHD.

33. Growth Mindset: The belief that talents, abilities, and intelligence can be developed and improved through dedication, effort, and learning, fostering grit, perseverance, and resilience in children with ADHD.

34. Neuroplasticity: The brain's ability to reorganize, adapt, and form new neural connections throughout life in response to learning, experience, and environmental stimuli, showcasing the brain's malleability and capacity for change in children with ADHD.

35. Self-Regulation: The ability to manage one's emotions, behaviors, and impulses effectively, demonstrating self-control, emotional regulation, and adaptability in different situations and contexts for children with ADHD.

36. Positive Parenting: A parenting approach that emphasizes warmth, support, clear communication, and consistent discipline to promote a strong parent-child bond, encourage independence, and nurture positive self-image and resilience in children with ADHD.

37. School Accommodations: Modifications, supports, or services provided by schools to address the specific learning, behavioral, or emotional needs of children with ADHD, ensuring access to academic opportunities, social inclusion, and educational success for children with ADHD.

38. Stress Management Techniques: Coping strategies, relaxation exercises, and mindfulness practices used to reduce stress, alleviate anxiety, and promote emotional well-being in children with ADHD, fostering resilience, self-regulation, and mental health.

39. Support Network: A system of individuals, professionals, and resources that provide

emotional support, guidance, and practical assistance to parents, caregivers, and children with ADHD, offering a sense of community, understanding, and advocacy.

40. Inclusive Education: An approach to education that ensures equal access, participation, and opportunities for all students, including those with ADHD, promoting diversity, equity, and support for individual learning needs and styles.

41. Emotional Intelligence: The ability to recognize, understand, manage, and express emotions effectively, as well as perceive and navigate the emotions of others, fostering self-awareness, empathy, and social skills in children with ADHD.

42. Behavioral Support: Strategies, interventions, and tools designed to address challenging behaviors, promote positive behavior, and teach coping skills,

problem-solving, and self-regulation to children with ADHD.

43. Learning Styles: Individual preferences and strengths in how children process information, acquire knowledge, and engage in learning, such as visual, auditory, kinesthetic, or a combination of learning styles that influence academic performance and engagement in children with ADHD.

44. Social-Emotional Development: The process of acquiring social skills, emotional awareness, and interpersonal abilities, which impact relationships, communication, and behavior in social contexts for children with ADHD.

45. Strengths-Based Approach: An approach that focuses on identifying, nurturing, and leveraging a child's strengths, interests, and talents to promote self-confidence, motivation, and success, emphasizing positive attributes and capabilities in children with ADHD.

46. Executive Function Skills: Cognitive skills that enable individuals to plan, organize, prioritize, initiate, sustain attention, manage time, and inhibit impulses, crucial for goal-directed behavior, problem-solving, and self-regulation in children with ADHD.

47. Peer Support: Positive relationships, social connections, and interactions with peers that provide emotional, social, and academic support, fostering a sense of belonging, collaboration, and friendship for children with ADHD.

48. Family Therapy: A form of counseling or therapy that involves family members in treatment, addressing dynamics, communication patterns, and relationships to improve understanding, cohesion, and support for children with ADHD and their families.

49. Positive Reinforcement: A behavior modification technique that involves rewarding desired behaviors, actions, or accomplishments to increase the likelihood of their recurrence,

reinforcing positive behaviors, motivation, and self-esteem in children with ADHD.

50. Mindful Parenting: A parenting approach that focuses on being present, attentive, nonjudgmental, and responsive to children's needs, promoting empathy, understanding, and emotional connection to enhance communication, discipline, and support for children with ADHD.

51. Emotional Regulation: The ability to manage and control emotions in various situations, enabling children with ADHD to express feelings appropriately, cope with stress, and regulate their emotional responses effectively.

52. Flexible Thinking: The capacity to adapt to change, consider multiple perspectives, and adjust strategies or responses as needed, fostering problem-solving skills, creativity, and resilience in children with ADHD.

53. Social Support: Emotional, practical, and informational assistance received from family, peers, educators, or community members, offering encouragement, guidance, and understanding to children with ADHD as they navigate challenges and transitions.

54. Positive Affirmations: Encouraging and validating statements that reinforce children's strengths, abilities, and efforts, cultivating self-confidence, motivation, and a positive self-image in children with ADHD.

55. Environmental Modifications: Adjustments, accommodations, or changes made to the physical, sensory, or social environment to support the needs of children with ADHD, promoting comfort, organization, and effective learning experiences.